A Walking Theology

Learning about God
by walking with Jesus

Alan Wagner

A Walking Theology

© Copyright Alan Wagner, 2014

143 Acutt Avenue, Rosehill, 4051 South Africa

alankwagner@gmail.com

ISBN: 978-0-620-63603-2

Cover design: Niki Wagner

Editorial assistance: Mark Krause and Niki Wagner

INTRODUCTION: *What is a "Walking Theology"?*

Theology is "the study of God" – discovering what he is like.

It is incredibly valuable to have a sound theology. A *poor* view of God can drive us away from him and move us to make poor life choices. A *good* view of God will draw us towards him and move us to make wise life choices.

The *challenge* with theology though, is that the harder we try to describe God adequately, the more likely we are to produce a book that is hard to understand! Have you ever picked up a theology book and been faced with a lot of words and concepts that you battled to understand? Have you bravely ploughed through such a book, but didn't gain the benefits you'd hoped for?

Although God is great beyond our understanding, *he has made himself known through Jesus to the degree that ordinary people can get to know him* – having what we could call a *"working theology"*. *This book is written with the goal of giving the reader a healthy, helpful, "working view" of God, regardless of academic capability.*

It is encouraging to know that most of Jesus' apostles were "unschooled". Luke records in Acts 4:13 that Peter and John were "unschooled, ordinary men" – but also noted they had been with Jesus. These were key men in the early church, but they were not academics – *they learned their theology from walking with Jesus.*

Jesus' words to the apostle Philip reveal this intention:

> *"Have I been with you all this time, Philip, and yet you still don't know who I am?* **Anyone *who has seen* me *has seen the* Father!** *So why are you asking me to show him to you?"*

> - John 14:9 (NLT)

When Philip asked Jesus to show God to him, Jesus told him that this is exactly what he had been doing over the past years – not by *lecturing* him, but by *living with* him.

The aim of this book is to present a helpful picture of God by observing Jesus through the eyes of the disciples. We'll do this by reading their personal stories recorded in the Gospels (primarily the Gospel of Luke). As we "walk with the disciples" and observe Jesus, we will get to know God better.

This book is also an invitation to "walk your own walk" with Jesus – to "walk out" each truth personally. You are invited to read a chapter, reflect on what you have learned, and then "walk it out" through the day or through the week. There is space provided for you to write down your personal "life lesson" – what you have learned or decided.

Please don't be intimidated by the number of chapters; the disciples' long walk has been broken up into many short "day trips" to help you to "walk at your own pace". Please don't rush through the book just to complete it – remember, the disciples had three years with Jesus! Some chapters may take you a day; others may need a week or longer. Take your time and allow these truths about God to deepen your relationship – and personal walk – with God.

Enjoy your walk!

Alan

CONTENTS: Looking ahead at the journey

1: God wants to be with us

The story of Jesus begins long before he was walking and talking with his disciples. It begins with something that is so remarkable it seems crazy! *God chooses to enter our world and live among us.* He chooses to take on flesh and blood, to be conceived in a woman's body, to be born and to grow up into adulthood as a son of an ordinary mother and father. God became flesh and dwelt amongst us!

John's gospel starts by marvelling at this:

> *In the beginning the Word already existed. The Word was with God, and the Word **was God**.*
>
> *...The Word gave life to everything that was created, and his life brought light to everyone.*
>
> *...So the Word **became human and made his home among us**. He was full of unfailing love and faithfulness. And we have seen his glory, the glory of the Father's one and only Son.*

- John 1:1, 4, 14 (NLT)

In his gospel, Matthew remembers the words of the prophecy of Isaiah spoken about 700 years before:

> *All of this occurred to fulfil the Lord's message through his prophet: "Look! The virgin will conceive a child! She will give birth to a son, and they will call him Immanuel, which means **'God is with us.'**"*

- Matthew 1:22-23 (NLT)

The theological term for this outrageous act of God is "incarnation" – God taking on flesh. Somehow, God entered our world in human flesh and blood. The invisible and intangible became visible and tangible. He lived life with us and revealed to us who God is.

So one of the first lessons we learn about God from Jesus is that GOD WANTS TO BE WITH US.

God is not content to be "God out there somewhere", or "the man upstairs"; he wants to be "God with us". He is not aloof, not too "high and mighty" to connect with us. God is not indifferent, not too busy with heavenly things to worry about you and I on earth.

God wants to *engage* – to *connect* – to *relate* – with you and I. He is relational and seeks relationship with us.

WALK IT:

Self-image

How does this change how you feel about yourself? Think about it; God left heaven for YOU!

Prayer

How does this change the way you pray? Here are some thoughts:

- Pray knowing that you have God's attention and interest.

- Spend time alone just seeking to enjoy God's company ("presence").

MY "LIFE LESSON":

2: God is interested in our "ordinary life"

And while they were there, the time came for her baby to be born. She gave birth to her first child, a son. She wrapped him snugly in strips of cloth and laid him in a manger, because there was no lodging available for them.

...Eight days later, when the baby was circumcised, he was named Jesus, the name given him by the angel even before he was conceived.

...When Jesus' parents had fulfilled all the requirements of the law of the Lord, they returned home to Nazareth in Galilee. There the child grew up healthy and strong. He was filled with wisdom, and God's favour was on him.

...Jesus grew in wisdom and in stature and in favour with God and all the people.

- Luke 2:6-7, 21, 39-40, 52 (NLT)

Have you ever wondered what happened in Jesus' life before he began what we call his "ministry" (the years when he was preaching and performing miracles)? Have you ever wondered why Jesus lived thirty years in relative obscurity before his three years of public "ministry"?

In one sense, it seems rather inefficient to live thirty "ordinary" years followed by three "high impact" years. But in another sense, it reveals something of the heart of God. He has time for "ordinary" living as well as extraordinary living. He has time for us "ordinary ones". Luke records that Jesus enjoyed favour with "all the people" during his "ordinary years" – in other words, he was popular. He was evidently not resentfully enduring ordinary human life until deemed old enough to preach. He was living his ordinary life well!

This is *not* to say we should "aspire to be ordinary"! Luke also records that God's favour was clearly on Jesus! That means that there was clearly visible evidence of God working in him in those "ordinary years".

God is interested in our "ordinary". He was prepared to live it for 30 years! And this is more than an academic interest; he wants to be *involved* in it; to show himself, his working and his favour in our lives. *Our lives matter to God. Our marriages, our families, our friendships, our work... they all matter to God.*

You may have been exposed to thinking that separates life into "secular" and "sacred" – meaning that God is interested in *some* parts of life ("sacred" – like church meetings) and disinterested in others ("secular" – like work). Jesus did not teach this; he showed the favour of God in "ordinary" life.

God is interested in ALL of your life!

WALK IT:

Prayer

Talk to God about the things you used to think were too insignificant for his attention (too small/personal/practical/"earthly").

View of work and daily life

- Rethink the value of your work (if God was happy to be a carpenter that surely gives work significance).

- Rethink your view of the so-called "sacred" and "secular"; are you excluding God from parts of your life because you thought he had no interest in them? How do you think he could he be involved in these things?

MY "LIFE LESSON":

3: God is righteous – and values what is right

Then Jesus came from Galilee to the Jordan to be baptised by John. But John tried to deter him, saying, 'I need to be baptised by you, and do you come to me?' Jesus replied, 'Let it be so now; it is proper for us to do this to fulfil all righteousness.' Then John consented.

As soon as Jesus was baptised, he went up out of the water. At that moment heaven was opened, and he saw the Spirit of God descending like a dove and alighting on him. And a voice from heaven said, 'This is my Son, whom I love; with him I am well pleased.'

- Matthew 3:13-17 (NIV)

Before Jesus began his ministry, he presented himself to John the Baptist for baptism. John knew who Jesus was, so felt that this was the wrong way round – like the student baptising the teacher or the follower baptising the master. Furthermore, his baptising Jesus could have presented Jesus as a repenting sinner.

But John's understanding was incomplete. It *was* right for Jesus to be baptised – not for the reasons the others had come to John (repentance), but to represent the beginning of his "priestly ministry". This was in a sense his "ordination", the ceremony announcing his transition from carpenter to rabbi and priest.

So, in spite of John's awkwardness and the potential for misunderstanding, Jesus "did the right thing" – "it is proper for us to do this to fulfil all righteousness".

And God affirmed his pleasure over his Son at that moment: "This is my Son, whom I love; with him I am well pleased."

WALK IT:

<u>Do the right thing</u>

Are you justifying not doing something that you *know* is right? Have you come up with some really good reasons not to do it? Is it perhaps "politically incorrect"? Could it perhaps be misunderstood and "paint you in a bad light"? Follow Jesus' example and do the right thing – this will please God!

MY "LIFE LESSON":

4: God understands our struggle with evil

Then Jesus, full of the Holy Spirit, returned from the Jordan River. He was led by the Spirit in the wilderness, where he was tempted by the devil for forty days. Jesus ate nothing all that time and became very hungry.

...When the devil had finished tempting Jesus, he left him until the next opportunity came.

- Luke 4:1-2, 13 (NLT)

So then, since we have a great High Priest who has entered heaven, Jesus the Son of God, let us hold firmly to what we believe. This High Priest of ours understands our weaknesses, for he faced all of the same testings we do, yet he did not sin. So let us come boldly to the throne of our gracious God. There we will receive his mercy, and we will find grace to help us when we need it most.

- Hebrews 4:14-16 (NLT)

Jesus' ministry was preceded by a head-on confrontation with the devil. The devil tried his best to tempt Jesus to disqualify himself by sinning against God – but failed. This was by no means the end of his temptation and the worst attack was surely the horrific series of events leading up to his crucifixion. Jesus was at times hungry, tired, sad, disappointed, frustrated, misunderstood, deserted and rejected – to name a few of our "stress factors".

God understands our trials and temptations!

Have you ever poured out your heart to someone and realised that they actually have no clue how you are feeling? It can be like that with people, but not with God. He has tasted the harshest realities of life on earth!

You can talk to God about struggles – he understands!

13

WALK IT:

Prayer

- Do you sometimes feel awkward coming to God when you are feeling tempted? That is when we most need to come to him! Take comfort in the knowledge that he "knows how it feels" – and he knows how to win your battle! "So let us come boldly to the throne of our gracious God. There we will receive his mercy, and we will find grace to help us when we need it most."

- Are you not talking to God about some areas of your life because you are ashamed of them and can't imagine him understanding your struggle? Talk to him about it!

Victory over sin

Sometimes we fail to overcome sin because we fail to talk to God when we are tempted. Remember, he understands temptation – he does not turn his back on us in disgust that we are being tempted!

If we disengage from him as if he is not present, we won't ask for his help. If we turn to him in the midst of temptation, we are engaging with the one who overcame every temptation!

[Note: if you are currently fighting temptation, it may help to jump to chapter 9: "God is more powerful than the devil".]

MY "LIFE LESSON":

5: God wants us to change – for the better

From that time on Jesus began to preach, 'Repent, for the kingdom of heaven has come near.'

- Matthew 4:17 (NIV)

We have seen that God wants to be with us… that he seeks relationship with us… that he came to us… and that he understands the challenges and temptations of life as we know it.

That can give us the idea that he is happy with our lives as we know it and does not expect us to change (that our unrighteousness is OK with him). But this is not true! Jesus frequently called people to repent (change the way they think about things) – and to change their actions accordingly.

For example, John 8:1-11 records a situation where Jesus dealt with a woman found guilty of adultery. He declared her released from condemnation, but also instructed her to change her ways:

'Then neither do I condemn you,' Jesus declared. 'Go now and leave your life of sin.'

- John 8:11 (NIV)

God *does* want to be with us. He *does* want an authentic relationship with us. But he does *not* abandon *his* ways and embrace *ours* in order to do so; instead he calls us to abandon *our* ways and embrace *his!* He calls us to change our way of thinking about the way we live – by learning and embracing his thinking.

This call to change is not in conflict with God's desire to enjoy a close relationship with him; he calls us to make changes *so that we can* enjoy that close relationship!

15

Mankind lost their close relationship with God in Eden because they chose their own way; Jesus calls us to return to God's ways and come back into the relationship we were made for!

WALK IT:

Making changes

Have you been challenged to make a change in an area of your life, but dismissed the challenge? Perhaps you dismissed it as "law – and I'm under grace" or as "old-fashioned, outdated rules"... perhaps you successfully justified your behaviour as "everyone does it", "that's how the game is played", or "it's perfectly acceptable in our day".

Look at the challenge again and ask: "What does the Bible say?" Based on the answer, ask: "Does God require me to make a change here?"

MY "LIFE LESSON":

6: God is kind, generous and excellent

*The next day there was a wedding celebration in the village of
Cana in Galilee. Jesus' mother was there, and Jesus and his
disciples were also invited to the celebration. The wine supply ran
out during the festivities, so Jesus' mother told him, "They have no
more wine."*

*...Standing nearby were six stone water jars, used for Jewish
ceremonial washing. Each could hold twenty to thirty gallons.
Jesus told the servants, "Fill the jars with water." When the jars
had been filled, he said, "Now dip some out, and take it to the
master of ceremonies." So the servants followed his instructions.
When the master of ceremonies tasted the water that was now
wine, not knowing where it had come from (though, of course, the
servants knew), he called the bridegroom over. "A host always
serves the best wine first," he said. "Then, when everyone has had
a lot to drink, he brings out the less expensive wine. But you have
kept the best until now!"*

- John 2:1-3, 6-10 (NLT)

Jesus' first recorded miracle was to discretely rescue a bridegroom
from the embarrassment of running out of wine at his wedding feast.
In this we see some magnificent aspects of the nature of God:

- **Kindness**: Jesus saved the bridegroom and his family from
significant embarrassment amongst their community. He did not
rescue them from serious sickness or grave danger, just from an
awkward situation. *This is very kind!*

- **Extravagant generosity**: Jesus provided the party with
somewhere between 450 and 680 litres of wine – way more than was
needed! The party could continue for as long as they wanted to!

- **Excellence**: Jesus did not just produce wine; he produced *the very
best* wine!

Here's another magnificent demonstration of the generosity of God:

When the apostles returned, they told Jesus everything they had done. Then he slipped quietly away with them toward the town of Bethsaida. But the crowds found out where he was going, and they followed him. He welcomed them and taught them about the Kingdom of God, and he healed those who were sick. Late in the afternoon the twelve disciples came to him and said, "Send the crowds away to the nearby villages and farms, so they can find food and lodging for the night. There is nothing to eat here in this remote place."

But Jesus said, "You feed them." "But we have only five loaves of bread and two fish," they answered. "Or are you expecting us to go and buy enough food for this whole crowd?" For there were about 5,000 men there. Jesus replied, "Tell them to sit down in groups of about fifty each." So the people all sat down. Jesus took the five loaves and two fish, looked up toward heaven, and blessed them. Then, breaking the loaves into pieces, he kept giving the bread and fish to the disciples so they could distribute it to the people.

They all ate as much as they wanted, and afterward, the disciples picked up twelve baskets of leftovers!

- Luke 9:10-17 (NLT)

In this miracle, we see God's control over natural elements, but we also see his extravagant generosity. This was a response to a reasonable need – the people needed to be fed – but God's response went way beyond "reasonable provision":

"They all ate as much as they wanted, and afterward, the disciples picked up twelve baskets of leftovers!"

This was not a rationed food queue! Everyone was free to eat as much as they liked. And then there were still leftovers! When we pray for provision, we should remember that we ask the One who is generous, who gladly provides more than enough.

18

WALK IT:

<u>Prayer</u>

How do you pray for provision? "God, just help me get by", or "Father, please provide plentifully so that we can be generous"? Why not ask God for some things that engage his kindness and generosity!

<u>Giving/hospitality</u>

Are you generous? Generosity is beautiful! Generosity reflects something of God! Next time you give to a beggar or a cause, why not surprise them? Next time you have guests, why not provide such that they take something home?

<u>Faith</u>

How do you see God? Do you see him as kind and generous? Does it surprise you that he cares about something like the wine supply at a wedding party? Spend time reflecting on these aspects of his nature and allow them to grow your expectations of him.

MY "LIFE LESSON":

7: God speaks – and what he says, he does!

[Jesus] went to Nazareth, where he had been brought up, and on the Sabbath day he went into the synagogue, as was his custom. He stood up to read, and the scroll of the prophet Isaiah was handed to him. Unrolling it, he found the place where it is written: 'The Spirit of the Lord is on me, because he has anointed me to proclaim good news to the poor. He has sent me to proclaim freedom for the prisoners and recovery of sight for the blind, to set the oppressed free, to proclaim the year of the Lord's favour.' Then he rolled up the scroll, gave it back to the attendant and sat down. The eyes of everyone in the synagogue were fastened on him. He began by saying to them, 'Today this scripture is fulfilled in your hearing.'

- Luke 4:16-21 (NIV)

The Old Testament is full of prophecies – words that God gave to men to speak on his behalf. Many of these prophecies foretold the coming Messiah – the one who would come to rescue Israel.

As Jesus read those words, this must have been a profound moment – because they spoke of *him*. As he read them, they were no longer words foretelling a future event; they had become *fulfilled* words!

God speaks to man. In this case, he spoke through the words of a prophet. In other cases recorded by the disciples, God spoke through angels, in dreams and even in an audible voice. He teaches. He affirms. He corrects. He even foretells events.

Isaiah prophesied about Jesus about 700 years before Jesus fulfilled his words. Many had hoped to see the words fulfilled, but they never did. Some people probably gave up on the promises; but God kept his word – in his time, not theirs.

So know this; God speaks and God speaks the truth. If he promises something, he will do it. It may take longer than we prefer, but he will do it – in his perfect timing!

WALK IT:

<u>Faith</u>

Are there promises you see in the Bible – or that you believe God has made to you though other means, such as dreams or prophetic words – that you have given up on? Dare to believe again... add patience to your faith:

> *...imitate those who through faith and patience inherit what has been promised.*

> - Hebrews 6:12 (NIV)

MY "LIFE LESSON":

8: God's ways can offend us deeply

"Certainly there were many needy widows in Israel in Elijah's time, when the heavens were closed for three and a half years, and a severe famine devastated the land. Yet Elijah was not sent to any of them. He was sent instead to a foreigner—a widow of Zarephath in the land of Sidon. And there were many lepers in Israel in the time of the prophet Elisha, but the only one healed was Naaman, a Syrian." When they heard this, the people in the synagogue were furious. Jumping up, they mobbed him and forced him to the edge of the hill on which the town was built. They intended to push him over the cliff, but he passed right through the crowd and went on his way.

- Luke 4:25-30 (NLT)

The Jewish people of the time took pride in being God's chosen nation. As such, some felt they had "first claim" on God's blessings. So when Jesus pointed to history and highlighted how God performed miracles for gentiles (non-Jews) and not for Jews, they were deeply offended – so much so that they wanted to kill Jesus.

It is worth noting that Jesus did not express an *opinion* here; he quoted *facts* as recorded in the *Scriptures*. This was *history*. The people were not offended by an opinion or an insult; they were offended by the *truth* of one of God's ways.

God's ways are not the same as ours. He even declared that through Isaiah:

"My thoughts are nothing like your thoughts," says the Lord. "And my ways are far beyond anything you could imagine. For just as the heavens are higher than the earth, so my ways are higher than your ways and my thoughts higher than your thoughts."

- Isaiah 55:8-9 (NLT)

God is bigger, better and way more clever than you and I! That may offend our pride, but it is one of the most important lessons we can ever learn. There will be times when God does something that offends us; for example when he does not fit in with our sense of justice or timing.

Our "theology" and our faith must always have room for mystery, for things we don't understand – because God is beyond our limited comprehension. Think about it: if God could be fully understood by mere human intellect, he would not be much of a God!!

God is God. We are not. He knows *more* than us, and he knows *better* than us. So there will be times when he mystifies us – let's make our peace with that!

WALK IT:

<u>Faith</u>

Has God offended you by failing to do what you expected him to or by doing what you never believed he would do? If he has, this could have done damage to your view of God.

These disappointing times are times to "enlarge" our view of God to allow for *mystery* – to embrace the tough realities that God does not think just like us and that God knows things we don't. That he knows better – and that his "better" does not always look better to us!

MY "LIFE LESSON":

9: God is greater than the devil

Once when he was in the synagogue, a man possessed by a demon—an evil spirit—began shouting at Jesus, "Go away! Why are you interfering with us, Jesus of Nazareth? Have you come to destroy us? I know who you are—the Holy One of God!" Jesus cut him short. "Be quiet! Come out of the man," he ordered. At that, the demon threw the man to the floor as the crowd watched; then it came out of him without hurting him further. Amazed, the people exclaimed, "What authority and power this man's words possess! Even evil spirits obey him, and they flee at his command!"

- Luke 4:33-36 (NLT)

Demon possession can be a terrible and a frightening thing. An evil power enters a person and begins to take charge of them... and it's a power greater than mere human power.

The good news is that Jesus never struggled with demons; not even in large numbers (read Luke 8:26-33). He knew his authority as God's representative. They were no match for him!

If the idea of a confrontation with the demonic scares you, know this: *it does not scare God!* He is *far* more powerful!

Jesus told his disciples:

I will build my church, and all the powers of hell will not conquer it.

- Matthew 16:18 (NLT)

The church is in conflict with the powers of hell… but take heart: those powers will *not* conquer it! *God is greater than the devil!*

WALK IT:

Faith

- Have you resigned yourself to evil around you – concluding that these are evil times and that's just the way it is? These *are* evil times – but *add* to that realisation the knowledge that God is greater than the devil and his demons – and that God takes them on and defeats them!

- Do you avoid situations that could place you in conflict with evil forces? This can keep you from doing things that God has prepared for you to do! Ask God to free you from fear of evil opposition so that you won't shrink back from what he has for you to do.

Combat strategy

James gives us this strategy to victory over the devil's schemes:

Submit yourselves, then, to God.

> *Resist* the devil, and he will flee from you.

> > *Come near* to God and he will come near to you.

> > > - James 4:7-8 (NIV)

Memorise this strategy and put it into practice next time you face temptation or evil opposition.

MY "LIFE LESSON":

10: God heals

After leaving the synagogue that day, Jesus went to Simon's home, where he found Simon's mother-in-law very sick with a high fever. "Please heal her," everyone begged. Standing at her bedside, he rebuked the fever, and it left her. And she got up at once and prepared a meal for them. As the sun went down that evening, people throughout the village brought sick family members to Jesus. No matter what their diseases were, the touch of his hand healed every one. Many were possessed by demons; and the demons came out at his command, shouting, "You are the Son of God!" But because they knew he was the Messiah, he rebuked them and refused to let them speak.

- Luke 4:38-41 (NLT)

This is a magnificent account of God's healing ways! It starts with a low-key healing in a home and ends with a public series of healings for the village. "No matter what their diseases were, the touch of his hand healed every one."

Don't you wish that was your experience? The bitter experience of many is that not everyone we pray for in the name of Jesus is healed. Why? We often don't know.

Sometimes it is related to lack of faith in Jesus. Matthew records a visit to Jesus' hometown (read Matthew 13:53-58). The people could not embrace Jesus for who he really was and they took offence at him. As a result, Matthew records, "he did not do many miracles there because of their lack of faith."

Other times, we can be confounded: we are full of faith, yet are disappointed. This is where we *really* need faith – when God does not meet our expectation!

26

Regardless of disappointments, we must know this: God *does* heal – and God is able to heal *any* disease. So let's bring the sick to him!

WALK IT:

Take Action

The gospel accounts show sick people coming to Jesus and people bringing the sick to Jesus. Let's be people who bring the sick to Jesus – and who come to him when we're sick. *God* is the one who heals, not us, so let's take the pressure off ourselves and leave it on God who heals!

MY "LIFE LESSON":

11: God is more than just our "personal God"

> *Early the next morning Jesus went out to an isolated place. The crowds searched everywhere for him, and when they finally found him, they begged him not to leave them. But he replied, "I must preach the Good News of the Kingdom of God in other towns, too, because that is why I was sent." So he continued to travel around, preaching in synagogues throughout Judea.*

> - Luke 4:42-44 (NLT)

The townsfolk must have slept lightly that night after the excitement of an evening of spectacular ministry. The town would have been buzzing with testimonies; people would probably have cancelled their plans for the next day just to get to see him! The next morning, a new crowd gathered for more – but Jesus had vanished! Some searched and eventually found him, but he had bad news for them: he was required elsewhere.

They must have been deeply disappointment. But God had different plans. There were many more towns that still needed this ministry; *they* needed an opportunity as well.

The townsfolk were probably focussed on *their* town, *their* sick friends and *their* needs – so they were naturally disappointed. But it was not that God didn't care about them; it's that *he saw others as well*. So Jesus moved on to reach the *others*.

Sometimes God disappoints us by not "getting with our program" – or by not "sticking to our program". We need to know that he sees further than we do, and trust him. We also need to know that he is not our "personal God"; he is *God over all*. Though his mission very much includes us, it goes way beyond us as well.

28

WALK IT:

Dealing with comparison

It is extremely likely that you know someone who has been blessed in a way that you have not. They were so-to-speak in that first crowd that all "got their miracles" – and you are in the second crowd that were told there would be no second meeting. It's disappointing. We can feel inferior or excluded. It's tempting to get jealous, even bitter.

It's also extremely likely that you have been blessed in some ways that others have not. It can be awkward. It can be tempting to get just a little proud or feel just a little more special.

Comparison is so dangerous; we'd best make every effort not to compare ourselves lest we become proud or bitter. We need to rather celebrate the Kingdom of God advancing wherever it is advancing at the time!

Dealing with the bigger picture

While the one town was sad to see Jesus go, the next town was *thrilled* to see him come! We need to learn to see beyond ourselves as God does – and celebrate the blessings of others even if we have not received the same blessing.

Sometimes we need to work harder so that others may rest; sometimes we need to sacrifice so that others may be blessed!

God's mission is the *world*; we *are* significant, but we need to make or peace with the reality that we are only *part* of the picture!

MY "LIFE LESSON":

12: God commands all nature

One day as Jesus was preaching on the shore of the Sea of Galilee, great crowds pressed in on him to listen to the word of God. He noticed two empty boats at the water's edge, for the fishermen had left them and were washing their nets. Stepping into one of the boats, Jesus asked Simon, its owner, to push it out into the water. So he sat in the boat and taught the crowds from there. When he had finished speaking, he said to Simon, "Now go out where it is deeper, and let down your nets to catch some fish."

"Master," Simon replied, "we worked hard all last night and didn't catch a thing. But if you say so, I'll let the nets down again."

And this time their nets were so full of fish they began to tear! A shout for help brought their partners in the other boat, and soon both boats were filled with fish and on the verge of sinking.

When Simon Peter realized what had happened, he fell to his knees before Jesus and said, "Oh, Lord, please leave me – I'm too much of a sinner to be around you."

- Luke 5:1-8 (NLT)

...At that time the highly valued slave of a Roman officer was sick and near death. When the officer heard about Jesus, he sent some respected Jewish elders to ask him to come and heal his slave.

...But just before they arrived at the house, the officer sent some friends to say, "Lord, don't trouble yourself by coming to my home, for I am not worthy of such an honour. I am not even worthy to come and meet you. Just say the word from where you are, and my servant will be healed. I know this because I am under the authority of my superior officers, and I have authority over my soldiers. I only need to say, 'Go,' and they go, or 'Come,' and they come. And if I say to my slaves, 'Do this,' they do it."

When Jesus heard this, he was amazed. Turning to the crowd that was following him, he said, "I tell you, I haven't seen faith like this in all Israel!" And when the officer's friends returned to his house,

30

they found the slave completely healed.

Soon afterward Jesus went with his disciples to the village of Nain, and a large crowd followed him. A funeral procession was coming out as he approached the village gate. The young man who had died was a widow's only son, and a large crowd from the village was with her. When the Lord saw her, his heart overflowed with compassion. "Don't cry!" he said.

Then he walked over to the coffin and touched it, and the bearers stopped. "Young man," he said, "I tell you, get up." Then the dead boy sat up and began to talk! And Jesus gave him back to his mother.

- Luke 7:1-15 (NLT)

One day Jesus said to his disciples, "Let's cross to the other side of the lake." So they got into a boat and started out. As they sailed across, Jesus settled down for a nap. But soon a fierce storm came down on the lake. The boat was filling with water, and they were in real danger. The disciples went and woke him up, shouting, "Master, Master, we're going to drown!" When Jesus woke up, he rebuked the wind and the raging waves. Suddenly the storm stopped and all was calm. Then he asked them, "Where is your faith?" The disciples were terrified and amazed. "Who is this man?" they asked each other. "When he gives a command, even the wind and waves obey him!"

- Luke 8:22-25 (NLT)

Simon was a fisherman by trade and knew how to fish. He was rightly puzzled that a rabbi should give him fishing advice; particularly when the advice was clearly pointless to him! In sheer obedience to Jesus, Simon let down the nets. When he saw the result, there was absolutely no doubt in his mind that a miracle had just taken place – *Jesus had just made a school of fish come to him!*

The Roman officer recognised the *immense authority* of Jesus. He lived in the military world where those in authority issued commands and those under authority obeyed. It was therefore easy for him to recognise Jesus as the "commander-in-chief" – so if Jesus issued the command for his slave to be healed, it would be so!

Jesus' next demonstration of his authority "pushed the envelope" even further – from healing a "near dead" servant to raising a "long dead" son back to life!

Then Jesus spoke into the elements of weather and stopped a raging storm. This rightly stunned his disciples; was there anything that Jesus did not command authority over?

In Genesis 1, we read of God commanding the entire natural world into being; in the gospels we read of God commanding it back into conformity with his will. God can do what we regard as "naturally impossible" because he still controls the "natural order" that he created!

WALK IT:

Prayer

Do you *really* believe that God can change *anything?* When you do, you will pray for anything and for any situation: from fishing to finances to physical and emotional healing, to rain! So look at situations around you. What do you believe is "out of order" (in terms of God's ways)? Start asking God to intervene in these situations, remembering that nothing is out-of-bounds for a miracle!

MY "LIFE LESSON":

13: God touches the untouchable

In one of the villages, Jesus met a man with an advanced case of leprosy. When the man saw Jesus, he bowed with his face to the ground, begging to be healed. "Lord," he said, "if you are willing, you can heal me and make me clean."

Jesus reached out and touched him. "I am willing," he said. "Be healed!" And instantly the leprosy disappeared.

- Luke 5:12-13 (NLT)

When we read this account, many focus in on the question of God's willingness to heal ("if you are willing"). Does God want to heal? Is healing important to God? Does he care about the suffering of the afflicted? The answer is surely a resounding YES!

But notice something else: *before* Jesus healed the man of his leprosy, he TOUCHED him. In those days, *no-one* touched a leper – both for health reasons (the risk of contracting the disease) and for religious reasons (they would be pronounced ceremonially "unclean").

Many people feel like "spiritual lepers" – that they are too "unclean" for God to care about them, much less to touch them. Jesus presents God as one who touches the untouchable.

No matter how "unclean" you think your past is… no matter how "unclean" you think you are at present… God is for you!

Let him touch you!

WALK IT:

Personal dirt

Is there an area of your life that you think is "untouchable" – something that is so repulsive that you could never present it to God? Think of this as "your leprosy" and bring it to God for his touch.

Relational dirt

Are there people who you avoid – or even refuse to be with – because there is something about them that repulses or offends you deeply? How do you think Jesus would treat them?

Next time you see them, make the effort to "break through the barrier" and do something that will show them the love and compassion that God has for them. For some people, this could be a life-changing moment – it may even lead them to faith in Jesus!

MY "LIFE LESSON":

14: God knows the depths of our hearts

Some men came carrying a paralyzed man on a sleeping mat. They tried to take him inside to Jesus, but they couldn't reach him because of the crowd. So they went up to the roof and took off some tiles. Then they lowered the sick man on his mat down into the crowd, right in front of Jesus. Seeing their faith, Jesus said to the man, "Young man, your sins are forgiven."

But the Pharisees and teachers of religious law said to themselves, "Who does he think he is? That's blasphemy! Only God can forgive sins!"

Jesus knew what they were thinking, *so he asked them, "Why do you question this in your hearts? Is it easier to say 'Your sins are forgiven,' or 'Stand up and walk'? So I will prove to you that the Son of Man has the authority on earth to forgive sins." Then Jesus turned to the paralyzed man and said, "Stand up, pick up your mat, and go home!" And immediately, as everyone watched, the man jumped up, picked up his mat, and went home praising God.*

- Luke 5:18-25 (NLT)

Behind this miracle of healing, we see something else about God: *he sees into our hearts and knows our thoughts.*

The Pharisees had not said a word, but Jesus knew what they were thinking. He knew there was a huge question in their hearts. So he articulated their unspoken question and answered it. It was an incredibly important question, as the answer would help the Jews to recognise their Messiah.

God knows our innermost thoughts!

Negatively, this means that there is no point in trying to kid God; we can conceal things from people, but not from God. God spoke this rebuke to Israel:

And so the Lord says, "These people say they are mine. They honor me with their lips, but their hearts are far from me. And their worship of me is nothing but man-made rules learned by rote."

- Isaiah 29:13 (NLT)

Positively, it means that he knows our deepest workings, even things we don't know how to express. So we can cry out to God – even when we are in total confusion – knowing that he understands what we mean! Paul the apostle put it like this:

And the Holy Spirit helps us in our weakness. For example, we don't know what God wants us to pray for. But the Holy Spirit prays for us with groanings that cannot be expressed in words. And the Father who knows all hearts knows what the Spirit is saying, for the Spirit pleads for us believers in harmony with God's own will.

- Romans 8:26-27 (NLT)

WALK IT:

<u>Prayer</u>

- Pray Psalm 139:23-24 (NLT): *"Search me, O God, and know my heart; test me and know my anxious thoughts. Point out anything in me that offends you, and lead me along the path of everlasting life."*

- Ask God to help you by his Spirit as you pray for inner pains, worries or fears that you don't understand, knowing that *he does* understand.

MY "LIFE LESSON":

15: God is not "religious"!

One Sabbath day as Jesus was walking through some grainfields, his disciples broke off heads of grain, rubbed off the husks in their hands, and ate the grain. But some Pharisees said, "Why are you breaking the law by harvesting grain on the Sabbath?"

Jesus replied, "Haven't you read in the Scriptures what David did when he and his companions were hungry? He went into the house of God and broke the law by eating the sacred loaves of bread that only the priests can eat. He also gave some to his companions." And Jesus added, "The Son of Man is Lord, even over the Sabbath."

On another Sabbath day, a man with a deformed right hand was in the synagogue while Jesus was teaching. The teachers of religious law and the Pharisees watched Jesus closely. If he healed the man's hand, they planned to accuse him of working on the Sabbath.

But Jesus knew their thoughts. He said to the man with the deformed hand, "Come and stand in front of everyone." So the man came forward. Then Jesus said to his critics, "I have a question for you. Does the law permit good deeds on the Sabbath, or is it a day for doing evil? Is this a day to save life or to destroy it?" He looked around at them one by one and then said to the man, "Hold out your hand." So the man held out his hand, and it was restored!

- Luke 6:1-10 (NLT)

Jesus offended the Pharisees on numerous occasions with his "irreligious" behaviour. The issue was never actually about breaking the *laws* given to Moses, but about not observing the "traditions of the elders" – the detailed instructions on *how to* observe the law. Jesus observed the *law*, but broke several *religious traditions*. In the eyes of the Pharisees, that made him a bad rabbi!

Here Luke records two Sabbath day conflicts. In terms of the law, the Sabbath was a day of rest where no-one was permitted to work. The religious leaders had an extensive list of things that they defined as "work", and *their list* was the source of the conflict.

In the first instance, the disciples ate grain from a field they were walking through. In the eyes of the Pharisees, this was "harvesting"; in the eyes of Jesus, this was hungry people having something to eat!

In the second instance, Jesus healed a man on the Sabbath. In the eyes of the Pharisees, this was "working"; in the eyes of Jesus, this was a good (and necessary) deed.

The religious Pharisees would have been happy for the disciples to have gone hungry for the sake of observing their traditions. Jesus was happy for the hungry disciples to have something to eat! Similarly, the Pharisees would have been happy for the man to remain crippled for the sake of their traditions; *but Jesus would have none of that!*

Some religious people do God a serious disfavour with their long lists of "thou shalt not..." rules – they give others the impression that God is miserably rule-driven like them!

Jesus showed us that God cares for people more than our man-made religious rules and regulations. *That's good news!*

WALK IT:

Review your view

How do you pray and worship? Do you have a "religious protocol" for approaching God? Do you observe rituals that you think are necessary to please God? Do you think God cares more about your religious behaviour than your well-being? Let Jesus correct your view of God.

MY "LIFE LESSON":

16: God is not impressed by religious ritual

As Jesus was speaking, one of the Pharisees invited him home for a meal. So he went in and took his place at the table. His host was amazed to see that he sat down to eat without first performing the hand-washing ceremony required by Jewish custom.

Then the Lord said to him, "You Pharisees are so careful to clean the outside of the cup and the dish, but inside you are filthy—full of greed and wickedness! Fools! Didn't God make the inside as well as the outside? So clean the inside by giving gifts to the poor, and you will be clean all over.

"What sorrow awaits you Pharisees! For you are careful to tithe even the tiniest income from your herb gardens, but you ignore justice and the love of God. You should tithe, yes, but do not neglect the more important things."

- Luke 11:37-42 (NLT)

Religious ritual is a strange thing. When centred on God, it can be incredibly meaningful and helpful (that's why God gave Israel some beautiful rituals to observe). But, over time, the ritual can become our focus – instead of the *reason* for it.

This Pharisee had got stuck on the ritual – so he was offended when Jesus didn't perform it. Jesus had to remind him that external washing represented the need for internal cleansing – and that giving was for the sake of justice and the love of God.

Some think that God requires a life of religious ritual – but it is godly living that *really* pleases him!

WALK IT:

<u>Attitude check</u>

- Do you think your church does some things better than others – better songs, service format etc? Or does it bother you that others don't do certain things "properly"?

- Do you feel guilty if you miss a prayer time or forget to say grace before a meal? If so you may be becoming "religious" in an unhelpful sense.

<u>Ritual check</u>

- Do you catch yourself "saying a prayer" or reading the Bible or a devotional and realise that "nothing went in"; you didn't really engage? You "did the right thing" but it was more of a ritual than engaging with God. Remind yourself of *why* you do these things and let that change the *way* you do them.

MY "LIFE LESSON":

17: God calls us to embrace new roles and responsibilities

One day soon afterward Jesus went up on a mountain to pray, and he prayed to God all night. At daybreak he called together all of his disciples and chose twelve of them to be apostles. Here are their names: Simon (whom he named Peter), Andrew (Peter's brother), James, John, Philip, Bartholomew, Matthew, Thomas, James (son of Alphaeus), Simon (who was called the zealot), Judas (son of James), Judas Iscariot (who later betrayed him).

- Luke 6:12-16 (NLT)

Over some time, Jesus had called numerous people to follow him as his disciples. One day, he called all of them together and called out twelve of them to be apostles.

For those twelve men, you could say this was a "second calling". Jesus had first called them to leave their vocations to become disciples; now he called them out to become apostles.

Why these twelve? There were probably some eyebrows raised as the names were called and their new role pronounced. Why choose an ex-revolutionary (Simon the zealot) and an ex-tax collector (Matthew)? Why fishermen and not potential rabbis? Jesus didn't explain. If asked, he would have probably said "because God said so" – after all, he had spent all night praying before calling the twelve. Regardless of all that, we see that God called them to take on a new role.

At various times, God calls various people to take on various roles. It is *his* call, not ours, and it may be surprising sometimes. When he does, remember that he knows what he is doing even if we don't! And remember that it is a *privilege to serve him as he calls us to*, not a position of status.

- He called these men to discipleship and then to apostleship.

- He called a man called Cornelius to contact Peter to bring the gospel to non-Jews (you can read about it in Acts chapter 10).

- He may call YOU to take on a new role in the future. If he does, embrace his call with your all!

WALK IT:

Openness

- Are you open to God calling you to a new role or responsibility?

- Are you open to God calling others to a new role or responsibility and not you?

Prayer

Ask God if he wants to make any changes in your life.

MY "LIFE LESSON":

18: God does not value our comfort like we may do

Then Jesus turned to his disciples and said, "God blesses you who are poor, for the Kingdom of God is yours. God blesses you who are hungry now, for you will be satisfied. God blesses you who weep now, for in due time you will laugh. What blessings await you when people hate you and exclude you and mock you and curse you as evil because you follow the Son of Man. When that happens, be happy! Yes, leap for joy! For a great reward awaits you in heaven. And remember, their ancestors treated the ancient prophets that same way."

- Luke 6:20-23 (NLT)

There is a school of thought that thinks that God values our comfort like we do. In "believing" circles, this can result in a belief that God's blessing is only upon us when things are going well for us.

This series of statements by Jesus reveals a *very* different way of thinking. Disciples who are poor, hungry, weeping, hated, excluded and mocked are actually *blessed!*

Jesus pointed his disciples to Israel's history – God's prophets, those chosen to hear his words and proclaim them, endured many trials. You can possibly look at your life or those of friends and see good people enduring bad things (and bad people enjoying good things).

In a similar vein, don't think that calamity comes to those with the greatest sin – Jesus made it very clear that this is not the case:

About this time Jesus was informed that Pilate had murdered some people from Galilee as they were offering sacrifices at the Temple. "Do you think those Galileans were worse sinners than all the other people from Galilee?" Jesus asked. "Is that why they suffered? Not at all! And you will perish, too, unless you repent of your sins and turn to God. And what about the eighteen people who died when the tower in Siloam fell on them? Were they the worst sinners in Jerusalem? No, and I tell you again that unless you repent, you will perish, too."

- Luke 13:1-5 (NLT)

Jesus made it clear to his disciples that troubles would come to them:

"I have told you all this so that you may have peace in me. Here on earth you will have many trials and sorrows. But take heart, because I have overcome the world."

- John 16:33 (NLT)

So don't lose heart when things go wrong – this does not equate to God turning his back on you!

WALK IT:

Review your view

- When things go wrong is your reflex to ask "what have I done wrong?" It is good to ask God the question "have I caused this?" ("Am I reaping what I sowed?"), but we shouldn't *assume* that we're the cause.

- When things go wrong is your reflex to ask "where is God?" – or do you call on him for help knowing that he has overcome the world?

MY "LIFE LESSON":

19: God makes the first move towards unspiritual, sinful people

Later, as Jesus left the town, he saw a tax collector named Levi sitting at his tax collector's booth. "Follow me and be my disciple," Jesus said to him. So Levi got up, left everything, and followed him. Later, Levi held a banquet in his home with Jesus as the guest of honour. Many of Levi's fellow tax collectors and other guests also ate with them. But the Pharisees and their teachers of religious law complained bitterly to Jesus' disciples, "Why do you eat and drink with such scum?" Jesus answered them,

"Healthy people don't need a doctor – sick people do. I have come to call not those who think they are righteous, but those who know they are sinners and need to repent."

- Luke 5:27-32 (NLT)

(For a similar event, you can also read Luke 19:1-10 which records Jesus inviting himself to lunch with a tax collector named Zacchaeus.)

Jewish tax collectors were regarded as absolute scum. They had "sold out" to collect taxes from their people for the Roman Empire – and they were notorious for being corrupt, taking too much tax and keeping it for themselves. So in the eyes of the super-religious Pharisees, they were not the kind of people to be associated with.

Jesus offended them totally by (1) calling a tax collector to be his disciple and (2) eating a meal with a group of tax collectors (sharing a meal spoke of embracing relationship).

Did this mean that he was endorsing their sin? NO! Jesus made it clear that they were sinners who needed to change. But Jesus did not wait for them to change; *he made the first move.*

When a relationship fails due to an offence, we usually expect the offender to make right with the offended person. In terms of our

46

relationship with God, we have offended him; but God makes the first move, inviting us to come into relationship with him. This is ultimately demonstrated by Jesus:

Now, most people would not be willing to die for an upright person, though someone might perhaps be willing to die for a person who is especially good. But God showed his great love for us by sending Christ to die for us while we were still sinners.

- Romans 5:7-8 (NLT)

WALK IT:

Your relationship with God

Do you feel that your sins make God reluctant to connect with you and/or use you for his glory?

Your relationship with others

Do you think it pointless talking to some people about Jesus because their lifestyle is too sinful?

MY "LIFE LESSON":

20: God shows compassion to the undeserving

"But to you who are willing to listen, I say, love your enemies! Do good to those who hate you. Bless those who curse you. Pray for those who hurt you. If someone slaps you on one cheek, offer the other cheek also. If someone demands your coat, offer your shirt also. Give to anyone who asks; and when things are taken away from you, don't try to get them back. Do to others as you would like them to do to you. If you love only those who love you, why should you get credit for that? Even sinners love those who love them!

"...Love your enemies! Do good to them. Lend to them without expecting to be repaid. Then your reward from heaven will be very great, and you will truly be acting as children of the Most High, for he is kind to those who are unthankful and wicked. You must be compassionate, just as your Father is compassionate."

- Luke 6:27-32, 35-36 (NLT)

To many of us, these words of Jesus seem totally unreasonable. Loving your enemies and taking time to pray for those who are causing you pain. Not standing up for your rights. Opening yourself to potential bad debt.

Whether you can do these things or not, this is *God's* heart. He loves everyone, laying his life down even for his enemies. He shows kindness to the ungrateful and the wicked. This explains the complaint of some that "life is unfair" and the common observation that some bad people prosper. God is graceful and compassionate towards those who do evil as well as those who do good.

What "us good guys" need to realise though, is that from the point of view of a perfectly holy God, we *all* do evil at times – even the "really good guys". So we *all* need his grace and kindness.

You could call this "unreasonable compassion" – but it is actually "essential compassion", because *we all need it!*

Please don't get cross with God for showing grace to those you regard as evil; rather be grateful that he shows *you* grace!

WALK IT:

Review your view

- When someone wrongs you, do you lean towards justice (demanding that wrongs be made right) or towards grace (overlooking the offence and moving on)?

- When you do wrong, do you feel you would be unwelcome in the presence of God or do you believe you can come to him for forgiveness?

Pray

- Think of people who have hurt you (or are hurting you) – and pray for them. Ask God if there is a good thing you could do in a bad situation.

MY "LIFE LESSON":

21: God is also just

"Do not judge others, and you will not be judged. Do not condemn others, or it will all come back against you. Forgive others, and you will be forgiven. Give, and you will receive. Your gift will return to you in full—pressed down, shaken together to make room for more, running over, and poured into your lap. The amount you give will determine the amount you get back."

- Luke 6:37-38 (NLT)

"When you are on the way to court with your adversary, settle your differences quickly. Otherwise, your accuser may hand you over to the judge, who will hand you over to an officer, and you will be thrown into prison. And if that happens, you surely won't be free again until you have paid the last penny."

- Matthew 5:25-26 (NLT)

God is gracious and compassionate – even towards the wicked – but he is also just. Reaping what we sow is a God-principle. Our actions DO have consequences – even though sometimes God may "moderate" (soften) them in his compassion.

Understanding God's grace and justice can be difficult because as humans we commonly think "either-or" – that you either get grace or you get justice. When we have been wronged, we want justice; when we have done wrong, we want grace – but in both cases, the other party wants the opposite!

God thinks "both-and" – he is graceful, and he is just!

How does God combine the two? The best example is the work of the cross; the cross of Christ is the ultimate picture of perfect justice and perfect grace. In perfect justice, God declared mankind guilty of sin, and deserving death. In perfect grace, God became flesh to represent mankind and took their penalty upon himself.

Completely embracing justice and grace together can be very difficult for us, but we must not allow our limitations to reduce our view of God. Remember that we are getting to know God whose ways are far greater than ours!

WALK IT:

Relationship Check

- Do you have a tendency to be critical of the people around you? Do you find yourself "handing down judgement" or writing people off because of their sin or some other failure?

- Do you have a tendency to avoid conflict by simply ignoring what is wrong?

- Is there someone you need to ask forgiveness from?

- Is there someone you need to extend forgiveness to?

- Is there a wrong you need to put right (e.g. admit you were at fault, make restitution for damages done, return something to its rightful owner)?

- Do you need to speak up in an unjust situation?

MY "LIFE LESSON":

22: God expects obedience

"So why do you keep calling me 'Lord, Lord!' when you don't do what I say? I will show you what it's like when someone comes to me, listens to my teaching, and then follows it. It is like a person building a house who digs deep and lays the foundation on solid rock. When the floodwaters rise and break against that house, it stands firm because it is well built. But anyone who hears and doesn't obey is like a person who builds a house without a foundation. When the floods sweep down against that house, it will collapse into a heap of ruins."

- Luke 6:46-49 (NLT)

As God teaches us how to live, he expects us to pay attention and do what he says. His words are not "suggestions to consider", but instructions to follow!

And the instructions are *helpful*. When we build God's way, the building stands firm; when we ignore his instructions and build *our* way, the building collapses. God is not a "celestial kill-joy" who wants to "cramp our style"; he is the designer of life who wants to *give* us style!

If you have a house built, you will want a builder who has taken time to learn the correct ways to build and builds accordingly. Likewise, when you build your life – your marriage, your family, your business etc. – you would be wise to learn the right ways and build accordingly. It makes absolute sense that the designer and creator of everything knows best how life works – yet some think they know better! That is surely both arrogant and stupid.

God knows how life works – and he teaches us how to live accordingly. The Bible has been called "the instruction manual for life" because it teaches us the "ways that work". It is therefore both logical and wise to "read the manual" and "follow the instructions"!

WALK IT:

Obedience check

This may be a tough challenge: is there an area of your life that you know is "out of line" with the "instruction manual"? Are you persisting in your preferred way knowing that God has taught otherwise? Make today the day that you make a change or start a process of change!

MY "LIFE LESSON":

23: God delights in our loving response to his love

One of the Pharisees asked Jesus to have dinner with him, so Jesus went to his home and sat down to eat. When a certain immoral woman from that city heard he was eating there, she brought a beautiful alabaster jar filled with expensive perfume. Then she knelt behind him at his feet, weeping. Her tears fell on his feet, and she wiped them off with her hair. Then she kept kissing his feet and putting perfume on them. When the Pharisee who had invited him saw this, he said to himself, "If this man were a prophet, he would know what kind of woman is touching him. She's a sinner!"

Then Jesus answered his thoughts. "Simon," he said to the Pharisee, "I have something to say to you." "Go ahead, Teacher," Simon replied. Then Jesus told him this story: "A man loaned money to two people—500 pieces of silver to one and 50 pieces to the other. But neither of them could repay him, so he kindly forgave them both, cancelling their debts. Who do you suppose loved him more after that?" Simon answered, "I suppose the one for whom he cancelled the larger debt."

"That's right," Jesus said. Then he turned to the woman and said to Simon, "Look at this woman kneeling here. When I entered your home, you didn't offer me water to wash the dust from my feet, but she has washed them with her tears and wiped them with her hair. You didn't greet me with a kiss, but from the time I first came in, she has not stopped kissing my feet. You neglected the courtesy of olive oil to anoint my head, but she has anointed my feet with rare perfume. "I tell you, her sins—and they are many—have been forgiven, so she has shown me much love. But a person who is forgiven little shows only little love."

- Luke 7:36-47 (NLT)

The woman in this account was well known for her immoral behaviour, so religious people like Simon kept her at a distance. But Jesus revealed a forgiveness that extended to those regarded as the worst of sinners – and the woman responded to his extravagant grace with extravagant adoration.

To Simon, this behaviour was highly inappropriate; to Jesus, this behaviour was *totally* appropriate: she had been forgiven much and she accordingly loved much!

Ironically, Simon *also* needed forgiveness – but because he compared himself with others whose sin was more obvious or was regarded by society as worse, he failed to appreciate the grace of God extended to him. As a result, he "loved little". He invited Jesus for dinner, but did not bother to extend any other courtesies to him.

WALK IT:

Worship Reflection

Spend some time reflecting on the forgiveness that God has extended to you through Jesus. Think back to some of your thoughts, attitudes and actions that you know were wrong. You may not have "committed the big sins" (as you see them), but you *have* sinned – and those sins brought about a separation between you and God.

Then reflect on the crucifixion of Christ. He did that for *you* – because you *needed* him to.

This is his awesome love for you! As best as you can, in your own way, thank him and "love him back"!

MY "LIFE LESSON":

24: God is practical

Then Jesus gave the following illustration: "Can one blind person lead another? Won't they both fall into a ditch? Students are not greater than their teacher. But the student who is fully trained will become like the teacher. "And why worry about a speck in your friend's eye when you have a log in your own? How can you think of saying, 'Friend, let me help you get rid of that speck in your eye,' when you can't see past the log in your own eye? Hypocrite! First get rid of the log in your own eye; then you will see well enough to deal with the speck in your friend's eye."

- Luke 6:39-42 (NLT)

It has been quipped that "common sense isn't common" – sometimes the best counsel is plain practical sense:

- If you can't see the way forward, don't try to take the lead.

- If you follow someone, you will end up where they do.

- If you struggle more than someone else in an area, you're not positioned to help them until you gain victory yourself.

These lessons probably don't have you gasping in amazement at their profound wisdom. They are not hard to understand. *Yet many of us make these mistakes!* Jesus took time to teach "life skills" – and the Bible is full of practical wisdom like this. It's because God cares about practical living!

Remember, our "ordinary living" matters to him. Some people think God only cares about what happens in the spiritual realm, but his "street level lessons" show otherwise!

WALK IT:

Think about your life right now. Are there situations and relationships that need help? Have you prayed, but they are not getting better?

Perhaps there are *practical* steps you need to take. Go back to "the manual" (the Bible) and see if there is practical advice there for you. It can be daunting to begin with, so if you are new to the Bible, ask someone who is familiar with its contents. You can also get hold of a "topic list" that points you to Bible passages that can help you in different situations (some Bibles include one).

To start learning God's practical wisdom, start by reading Matthew chapters 5-7 (they record many powerful life-lessons) and the book of Proverbs (which is packed with practical wisdom).

MY "LIFE LESSON":

25: God's kindness can seem unfair

Jesus taught this parable:

"For the Kingdom of Heaven is like the landowner who went out early one morning to hire workers for his vineyard. He agreed to pay the normal daily wage and sent them out to work.

"At nine o'clock in the morning he was passing through the marketplace and saw some people standing around doing nothing. So he hired them, telling them he would pay them whatever was right at the end of the day. So they went to work in the vineyard. At noon and again at three o'clock he did the same thing.

"At five o'clock that afternoon he was in town again and saw some more people standing around. He asked them, 'Why haven't you been working today?' "They replied, 'Because no one hired us.' "The landowner told them, 'Then go out and join the others in my vineyard.'

"That evening he told the foreman to call the workers in and pay them, beginning with the last workers first. When those hired at five o'clock were paid, each received a full day's wage. When those hired first came to get their pay, they assumed they would receive more. But they, too, were paid a day's wage. When they received their pay, they protested to the owner, 'Those people worked only one hour, and yet you've paid them just as much as you paid us who worked all day in the scorching heat.'

"He answered one of them, 'Friend, I haven't been unfair! Didn't you agree to work all day for the usual wage? Take your money and go. I wanted to pay this last worker the same as you. Is it against the law for me to do what I want with my money? Should you be jealous because I am kind to others?'

"So those who are last now will be first then, and those who are first will be last."

- Matthew 20:1-16 (NLT)

58

The complaint of the first group of workers is understandable: they worked 12 hours and received the same pay as others who worked one! They cried "unfair!" But the landowner said, "No, I am being *kind!*" It was not that he had paid the first group badly; he had paid them correctly. The latter groups were simply privileged to receive a very generous payment.

God shows great kindness to people, sometimes to a degree that seems totally "unfair" – because it is totally undeserved. Forgiveness is probably the greatest example: he forgives people who have committed great atrocities in the same way as he forgives those who have not, calling us both his children.

When we see this "disproportionate kindness" happening, don't cry "unfair"; rather marvel at the amazing grace and kindness of God. Chances are you have been blessed more than some others – probably more than once!

WALK IT

Where are you on the farm?

Apply this parable to your life. Do you see yourself as one who works harder than others who earn more money or receive greater recognition? Has this made you jealous of them? Or even resentful? Has this affected your relationships?

Consider others around you. Are there people you haven't even noticed who are working even harder for less? Could they be envying you?

Economics God's way

How do *you* think God should reward us?

- In proportion to our "output" or "performance"? (So when we don't do so well, there's less blessing?) What about when things go wrong outside of our control?

- Should we all be blessed to the exact same extent always? (So the blessing is the same for all, no matter how well we're doing and how hard we're working?)

- Should there be room for graceful, "because I love you and I'm generous" blessings from God?

These questions are simply intended to help you realise that it's not a simple matter!

Let's rather be grateful that God is sometimes outrageously kind and generous – because one day we will surely need this!

MY "LIFE LESSON":

26: God is glorious and eternal

About eight days later Jesus took Peter, John, and James up on a mountain to pray. And as he was praying, the appearance of his face was transformed, and his clothes became dazzling white. Suddenly, two men, Moses and Elijah, appeared and began talking with Jesus. They were glorious to see. And they were speaking about his exodus from this world, which was about to be fulfilled in Jerusalem.

- Luke 9:28-31 (NLT)

This event was a mind-blowing revelation of God for the three disciples. They saw something of Jesus' glorious nature as his appearance was transformed into dazzling light!

And then they saw Moses and Elijah with him! Both of these men had died a long time ago – and they had lived at different times. So this event was "off the charts" of time! As the disciples gained a glimpse beyond the human body of Jesus to the glorious Son of God, they also gained a glimpse of Jesus' "normal world" – eternity!

John records a conversation with a group of Jewish people that turned ugly as Jesus presented his eternal nature:

"...Your father Abraham rejoiced as he looked forward to my coming. He saw it and was glad."

The people said, "You aren't even fifty years old. How can you say you have seen Abraham?"

Jesus answered, "I tell you the truth, before Abraham was even born, I am!"

- John 8:56-58 (NLT)

This was deeply offensive to the Jews – not just because he claimed to pre-date Abraham. The greater offence for them was that he was identifying himself as the one who is "eternally present", using the name that God had used to introduce himself to Moses: "I AM" (read about this is Exodus 3:14).

God is not trapped by space and time as we are. He is eternal. He is in our past and he is in our future! He is gloriously transcendent (going way beyond) of life as we know it!

Our view of God can be restricted by our limited view of "life as we know it". When we think of God in terms of space and time as we know it, this will be a view that is insultingly far beneath him!

WALK IT:

Nasty shocks and future fears

Has something taken you completely by surprise recently – you never saw it coming? It is comforting to know that it did not take God by surprise! You may be in shock, dazed and confused, but God is certainly not!

Do you fear certain unknowns in the future? It is comforting to know that our eternal God is already there!

Put your trust in I AM – in God who is "eternally present". Commit yourself and your situation to him, knowing that he knows your past, present *and* future!

MY "LIFE LESSON":

27: God is sacrificial – in love and life

Then he said to the crowd, "If any of you wants to be my follower, you must turn from your selfish ways, take up your cross daily, and follow me. If you try to hang on to your life, you will lose it. But if you give up your life for my sake, you will save it. And what do you benefit if you gain the whole world but are yourself lost or destroyed?"

- Luke 9:23-25 (NLT)

"Whoever wants to be a leader among you must be your servant, and whoever wants to be first among you must become your slave. For even the Son of Man came not to be served but to serve others and to give his life as a ransom for many."

- Matthew 20:26-28 (NLT)

"This is my commandment: Love each other in the same way I have loved you. There is no greater love than to lay down one's life for one's friends."

- John 15:12-13 (NLT)

Beyond generosity, God is *sacrificial*. We see that most profoundly in Jesus leaving heaven to come to earth – and then offering his life for the sins of mankind.

Because he is the ultimate demonstration of sacrificial love, God has every right to expect us to do likewise. If we want to *follow* him, we have to learn to give up our "me first" selfishness and lay down our personal priorities.

To respond correctly can be challenging, especially if we live in a selfish culture and have been taught to "look after number one". But the more we recognise the unselfish, sacrificial love of God, the more we gaze in awe at the magnificence of this "no greater love", the easier this becomes.

WALK IT:

Reflection

Spend time reflecting on the sacrifice God made for you: the Father releasing the Son to take on the sin of the world – and your sin; the Son leaving the Father and the glory of heaven to live as a man and die the cruellest death for the sin of the world – and your sin. And God did all this while we were living in disobedience!

Consider what your appropriate response should be as you seek to follow him.

Prayer

Ask God to reveal the enormity of his sacrifice for you. Ask him to show you if you are holding on to anything that is keeping you from following him closely.

Action

Jesus said he came to serve the world; consider how you can follow his example and serve!

MY "LIFE LESSON":

28: God has grace even for his enemies

As the time drew near for him to ascend to heaven, Jesus resolutely set out for Jerusalem. He sent messengers ahead to a Samaritan village to prepare for his arrival. But the people of the village did not welcome Jesus because he was on his way to Jerusalem. When James and John saw this, they said to Jesus, "Lord, should we call down fire from heaven to burn them up?" But Jesus turned and rebuked them. So they went on to another village.

- Luke 9:51-56 (NLT)

There was considerable animosity between Jews and Samaritans, so this probably contributed to the vengeful suggestion of James and John. But Jesus did not repay their rejection with wrath; he simply moved on. And Luke later recorded Jesus' parting words to the apostles that they would soon reach out to the people of Samaria with the Gospel (see Acts 1:8).

This is a wonderful picture of the grace of God. People reject him, but he continues to love them – and even pursues them!

A spectacular example of this grace is Saul – who later became known as Paul the apostle. Saul was once a bitter enemy of Jesus and the church, violently persecuting Jesus' followers. But Jesus rescued him regardless of all he had done, and he became one of the most powerful apostles in church history!

Some people think that God could not possibly accept them, because they have previously rejected him. If you are one of those people, gaze at the amazing grace of God and take heart – he still loves you!

WALK IT:

Reflection

- Are you carrying guilt or shame for past words or actions against Jesus that makes you feel that he would not want you? What does this aspect of God's grace show you?

- Have you "written someone off" because of their previous rejection of the Gospel? Pray for them. Ask God to correct your view of them and re-open your heart to talking to them about Jesus again.

MY "LIFE LESSON":

29: God is patient with the "non-performer"

Then Jesus told this story:

"A man planted a fig tree in his garden and came again and again to see if there was any fruit on it, but he was always disappointed. Finally, he said to his gardener, 'I've waited three years, and there hasn't been a single fig! Cut it down. It's just taking up space in the garden.

"The gardener answered, 'Sir, give it one more chance. Leave it another year, and I'll give it special attention and plenty of fertilizer. If we get figs next year, fine. If not, then you can cut it down.'"

- Luke 13:6-9 (NLT)

This is a story of justice; justice must – and will – be done. In this case, watering a tree for three years without any fruit already seems patient. But God adds a fourth year (time) as well as extra care (graceful intervention) before finally judging the tree fruitless.

Many believers are trophies of this patient grace of God: people who have resisted Jesus' offer of salvation for years... or persisted in disobedience for years... or resisted his call for years. Other people quite likely wrote them off, *but God did not.*

This is a magnificent patience!

Jesus demonstrated the same patience with his disciples. Many modern managers would have had Peter on "performance review" for trying to obstruct Jesus from fulfilling his mission (read Matthew 16:21-23). Many would have dismissed him outright for denying him three times (read Matthew 26:69-75). But Jesus persisted with him – and Peter fulfilled his destiny of becoming a pillar in the early church.

67

WALK IT:

<u>Patience with others</u>

Do you tend to write people off when they fail? Follow Jesus' example and learn patience.

<u>Patience with yourself</u>

Have you written yourself off – or have others written you off – because of a failure of some sort? Remember that God is the God of second chances and extra time. Come to him for forgiveness and restoration – and get back to walking into your destiny!

MY "LIFE LESSON":

30: God offers grace now; but his judgement will come

"But if a town refuses to welcome you, go out into its streets and say, 'We wipe even the dust of your town from our feet to show that we have abandoned you to your fate. And know this—the Kingdom of God is near!' I assure you, even wicked Sodom will be better off than such a town on judgment day.

"What sorrow awaits you, Korazin and Bethsaida! For if the miracles I did in you had been done in wicked Tyre and Sidon, their people would have repented of their sins long ago, clothing themselves in burlap and throwing ashes on their heads to show their remorse. Yes, Tyre and Sidon will be better off on judgment day than you."

- Luke 10:10-14 (NLT)

The grace of God towards his enemies is beautiful to some, but it offends others who ask if this is not abandoning justice. But the day of judgement *will* come, and justice *will* be completed at the end of the world as we know it.

Genesis chapters 18 and 19 record the destruction of the city of Sodom; it was destroyed by God for their shocking, all-prevading sinfulness. The people of Korazin and Bethsaida had rejected Jesus when he visited them with his message of redemption and a powerful demonstration of the grace and power of God. Because there was no immediate judgement upon them, they thought they were "ok". But Jesus assured them that they would answer for this on the day of judgement.

God *is* just, and we should not allow the generous extent of his present grace to blind us to his justice. If we do, this can lull us into complacency about the eternal fate of both ourselves and those around us. Let's heed his warning!

WALK IT:

Reflection

- Few of us like to think about subjects like "judgement day", hell and eternal punishment. But it is good that we do so from time to time, as it unsettles us from our complacency or denial. It motivates us to reach out to others. Take some time to reflect on these realities.

- It can be hard when we see people doing wrong and getting away with it. Is it worth doing the right thing when no-one seems to care? Read Psalm 73 for a rich expression of this question – and the answer.

MY "LIFE LESSON":

31: God values our company even more than our service

As Jesus and the disciples continued on their way to Jerusalem, they came to a certain village where a woman named Martha welcomed him into her home. Her sister, Mary, sat at the Lord's feet, listening to what he taught. But Martha was distracted by the big dinner she was preparing. She came to Jesus and said, "Lord, doesn't it seem unfair to you that my sister just sits here while I do all the work? Tell her to come and help me." But the Lord said to her, "My dear Martha, you are worried and upset over all these details! There is only one thing worth being concerned about. Mary has discovered it, and it will not be taken away from her."

- Luke 10:38-42 (NLT)

God is relational. He enjoys our company. This account demonstrates his priority of relationship over service as he corrects Martha. She is "doing good" in preparing a meal for Jesus and the other guests, but Mary was doing something *even more significant*: sitting and enjoying the company of Jesus.

Some wise person put it like this:

The Lord of the work is more important than the work of the Lord.

It is possible to get more caught up with "the things of God" than with God himself; that does not please him. Even this study could be done as an academic exercise – please allow it to direct you to prioritise spending time in his company!

WALK IT:

<u>Reflection</u>

- Are you more like Mary or Martha? Do you instinctively get to work on whatever needs to be done? Do you love times of worship and prayer? Are you able to "just sit" in God's presence?

- Have you been taught that "a person's actions are what really count" – that it is more to the point to *do* something about a situation than pray about it? Has this kind of thinking caused you to value working for God more than relationship with him?

<u>Prayer</u>

Spend some time worshipping God. Then spend some time "just sitting" in God's presence, just enjoying being his child. Don't "do", just "be" for a while.

MY "LIFE LESSON":

32: As a father, God values and responds to our prayers

Once Jesus was in a certain place praying. As he finished, one of his disciples came to him and said, "Lord, teach us to pray, just as John taught his disciples." Jesus said, "This is how you should pray: "Father, may your name be kept holy. May your Kingdom come soon. Give us each day the food we need, and forgive us our sins, as we forgive those who sin against us. And don't let us yield to temptation.

"...And so I tell you, keep on asking, and you will receive what you ask for. Keep on seeking, and you will find. Keep on knocking, and the door will be opened to you.

"...You fathers—if your children ask for a fish, do you give them a snake instead? Or if they ask for an egg, do you give them a scorpion? Of course not! So if you sinful people know how to give good gifts to your children, how much more will your heavenly Father give the Holy Spirit to those who ask him?"

- Luke 11:1-4, 9, 11-13 (NLT)

Jesus spoke a great deal about prayer:

- He taught his disciples *how* to pray.

- He taught them to pray *to* their Heavenly Father.

- He taught them to *persist* in praying when they feel "it's not working".

- He reminded them that God is the ultimate *father* and therefore the ultimate *source* of good gifts.

He taught all these things because prayer is really important to God! God is our Heavenly Father who delights to bless his children as they come to him in prayer, seeking his presence, his will and his blessing.

Prayer can sometimes feel like, or become a ritual. When we realise how God feels about our prayers, this changes! We are speaking to our Heavenly Father who is so glad to hear from us!

WALK IT:

<u>Prayer</u>

- How do you address God – and how do you think of him? Do you call him "Father"? Do you think of him as your Father? Engage Father in prayer for something that is really important to you – and as you do so, remember who he is: your Heavenly Father who knows how to give you good gifts!

- Have you prayed for someone or something and given up because nothing changed? Heed Jesus' call to be persistent in prayer and pray again.

MY "LIFE LESSON":

33: God values us highly!

"What is the price of five sparrows – two copper coins? Yet God does not forget a single one of them. And the very hairs on your head are all numbered. So don't be afraid; you are more valuable to God than a whole flock of sparrows."

- Luke 12:6-7 (NLT)

There are times when we can feel really insignificant.

- This is a really big world; we are one little person in a big crowd!

- "Super-stars" abound to intimidate us.

- Critics abound to unnerve us.

We can fall into the trap of putting those feelings on God – then we will end up thinking that we are surely insignificant to him.

A sparrow is a seemingly insignificant little bird – but even sparrows are remembered by God. So we need never feel that we are insignificant to God – he cares deeply about us!

Think about this: God is so interested in you that he knows how many hairs are on your head – information that no-one else but you would care about!

God's vision is truly amazing – he sees the biggest picture and the tiniest detail.

And he sees you!

WALK IT:

Self-image

While some people go through life self-confident, "backing themselves", others don't. Some live with inferiority complexes, broken down by negative words and actions; others just suffer from nagging self-doubts. Many cultures assign value to a person in terms of their looks, strengths, class, earnings or achievements – so some feel like "little people" – pretty much insignificant.

If this is you, it could be a struggle to see yourself as significant to God. You may need to spend some time reading and re-reading these words of Jesus until God's words overwhelm the legacy of many negative words and thoughts.

Please do. *You are worth it!*

Respect for others

Do you treat "little people" and "superstars" differently? Read Luke 14:8-14 and allow Jesus to challenge your thinking and actions!

MY "LIFE LESSON":

34: God requires our allegiance – even at a cost

"I have come to set the world on fire, and I wish it were already burning! I have a terrible baptism of suffering ahead of me, and I am under a heavy burden until it is accomplished. Do you think I have come to bring peace to the earth? No, I have come to divide people against each other! From now on families will be split apart, three in favour of me, and two against – or two in favour and three against."

- Luke 12:49-52 (NLT)

"Dear friends, don't be afraid of those who want to kill your body; they cannot do any more to you after that. But I'll tell you whom to fear. Fear God, who has the power to kill you and then throw you into hell. Yes, he's the one to fear."

- Luke 12:4-5 (NLT)

Following Jesus means being different from others who are *not* following him – so separation and conflict of some sort is inevitable.

When a person in a family of no faith – or of nominal faith – decides to follow Jesus, it is not as shocking as when one in a family of devout faith converts. The latter case can be traumatic. Families can be split apart. Some are cast out of their family and community; others even pay with their lives.

So while Jesus brings us into peace with *God*, this can bring us into severe conflict with *other people* – even people close to us. This is not because we have become *bad* (in some communities the convert is viewed in an extremely negative light), but because we have become *different*.

All of this can come as a shock – so Jesus warns us of these possibilities. There will inevitably be some price to pay for our faith.

You may be tempted to draw back from following Jesus because of the possible price. But remember, the eternal consequences are even more profound!

WALK IT:

Standing up for Jesus

Have you been avoiding making a decision to follow Jesus – or make him known – because you don't want to offend or cause strife? What does he ask of you?

Enduring persecution

Are you facing some sort of persecution for your faith in Jesus? Take comfort in two things: that Jesus warned you that this would happen, and that the eternal consequences are far more significant than the present ones. Consider this perspective from Paul:

> *That is why we never give up. Though our bodies are dying, our spirits are being renewed every day. For our present troubles are small and won't last very long. Yet they produce for us a glory that vastly outweighs them and will last forever! So we don't look at the troubles we can see now; rather, we fix our gaze on things that cannot be seen. For the things we see now will soon be gone, but the things we cannot see will last forever.*

> - 2 Corinthians 4:16-18 (NLT)

MY "LIFE LESSON":

35: God does not despise small beginnings

Then Jesus said, "What is the Kingdom of God like? How can I illustrate it? It is like a tiny mustard seed that a man planted in a garden; it grows and becomes a tree, and the birds make nests in its branches."

He also asked, "What else is the Kingdom of God like? It is like the yeast a woman used in making bread. Even though she put only a little yeast in three measures of flour, it permeated every part of the dough."

- Luke 13:18-21 (NLT)

Like a great tree grows from a small seed, God makes big things out of small things and great people out of "little people".

Like a little yeast makes a large batch of dough rise, he uses little things and "little people" to have great impact.

The prophet Zechariah spoke this word of encouragement to Israel many years before as a man named Zerubbabel started the daunting task of rebuilding the temple:

Do not despise these small beginnings, for the Lord rejoices to see the work begin, to see the plumb line in Zerubbabel's hand."
[Note: a plumb line is used to provide a true vertical reference as one begins building.]

- Zechariah 4:10 (NLT)

Sometimes we feel small, inadequate, insignificant and insufficient. But even if we are absolutely correct in our assessment, God can still use us to do great things!

WALK IT:

<u>Take the first step</u>

Do you have a dream of doing something really significant for God –
but it seems too big for you? Take the first step towards it. Do
something, even if it seems small: e.g. write down the dream, share it
with a leader, learn a skill that you'd need, or "make a small start"
(e.g. if you dream of playing stadium concerts, play in a low-key
event or venue).

MY "LIFE LESSON":

36: God mourns the necessary judgement

"O Jerusalem, Jerusalem, the city that kills the prophets and stones God's messengers! How often I have wanted to gather your children together as a hen protects her chicks beneath her wings, but you wouldn't let me."

- Luke 13:34 (NLT)

But as he came closer to Jerusalem and saw the city ahead, he began to weep. "How I wish today that you of all people would understand the way to peace. But now it is too late, and peace is hidden from your eyes. Before long your enemies will build ramparts against your walls and encircle you and close in on you from every side. They will crush you into the ground, and your children with you. Your enemies will not leave a single stone in place, because you did not recognize it when God visited you."

- Luke 19:41-44 (NLT)

Because God is just, there are times when he must execute justice – but this is done with pain. He longs to protect us, but we can refuse to come into his protection – and in due time, we will pay the price.

Some see God as angry and vengeful – as we perhaps are when despised, rejected and abused.

Others see him as detached and coldly judgemental – as a human judge is called to be – coldly sentencing the guilty to death.

But Jesus *wept* over his stubborn nation! He *mourned* their refusal to come into his loving protection which he likened to a mother hen who would gather her chicks under her wings to protect them.

Times of justice must come at times on earth – and final judgement will come as well. But know this: the judge longs for the guilty to receive his offer of mercy through Jesus!

81

WALK IT:

Grow your compassion

Think about someone – or a group of people – who is/are stubbornly refusing to acknowledge God and his offer of salvation. Maybe they are outspoken against him. Perhaps they arrogantly flaunt their sin. Ask God to give you some of his compassion for them – even enough that you would weep for them!

Then start praying for them, and ask God to show you if there is something that you can do to show them his enduring love for them in some way. If you have the opportunity, tell them of God's compassion for them.

MY "LIFE LESSON":

37: God demands his place as God

A large crowd was following Jesus. He turned around and said to them, "If you want to be my disciple, you must hate everyone else by comparison – your father and mother, wife and children, brothers and sisters – yes, even your own life. Otherwise, you cannot be my disciple. And if you do not carry your own cross and follow me, you cannot be my disciple.

"But don't begin until you count the cost. For who would begin construction of a building without first calculating the cost to see if there is enough money to finish it?"

- Luke 14:25-28 (NLT)

These are *really* strong words! If we heard of a religious leader demanding this degree of priority, we'd quite likely say that it was a very dangerous cult in the making! Surely no man can ever make this demand?

But this was no ordinary man – this was God made flesh. Only God could ever rightfully demand this level of priority – because as God, this place is rightfully his! Essentially, Jesus was saying that he cannot be our "number two" – because our "number one" is our true God. So what we are hearing is simply God demanding his rightful place!

Jesus later threw out a similar challenge:

"No one can serve two masters. For you will hate one and love the other; you will be devoted to one and despise the other. You cannot serve both God and money."

- Luke 16:13 (NLT)

There can only be one "number one"! Inevitably, we will have to choose who (or what) our ultimate master is.

Our allegiance to God is only tested when there is a price to pay. When family threaten to disown us for our faith... when our reputation is at risk... when there is a significant sacrifice to be made... These are times when our priority is truly tested; who (or what) is most important to us?

So Jesus called his would-be followers to think carefully before declaring him their Master – because at some stage, their allegiance would be tested.

It is logical that if God is really God, he should be "number one". But he understands that loving the invisible God more than our visible family and tangible life is a challenge... so he asks us to "process this" in our hearts and minds. *Then* we can be wholeheartedly submissive to him.

It is comforting to see God's many graces as we process this; when we see attributes such as his love, kindness, generosity and grace, we can submit to him confidently and with a real sense of security. God is God and God is good!

WALK IT:

Count the cost

Spend some time reflecting on possible prices you could pay for your faith. Rejection from friends or family? Ridicule? Loss of business or other income? Loss of your home? Loss of life?

Can you pay that price? It's a challenging question! Does this reveal competition for the "number one" position?

MY "LIFE LESSON":

38: God is the ultimate father

Tax collectors and other notorious sinners often came to listen to Jesus teach. This made the Pharisees and teachers of religious law complain that he was associating with such sinful people – even eating with them!

So Jesus told them this story: "If a man has a hundred sheep and one of them gets lost, what will he do? Won't he leave the ninety-nine others in the wilderness and go to search for the one that is lost until he finds it? And when he has found it, he will joyfully carry it home on his shoulders. When he arrives, he will call together his friends and neighbours, saying, 'Rejoice with me because I have found my lost sheep.' In the same way, there is more joy in heaven over one lost sinner who repents and returns to God than over ninety-nine others who are righteous and haven't strayed away!

"Or suppose a woman has ten silver coins and loses one. Won't she light a lamp and sweep the entire house and search carefully until she finds it? And when she finds it, she will call in her friends and neighbours and say, 'Rejoice with me because I have found my lost coin.' In the same way, there is joy in the presence of God's angels when even one sinner repents."

To illustrate the point further, Jesus told them this story: "A man had two sons. The younger son told his father, 'I want my share of your estate now before you die.' So his father agreed to divide his wealth between his sons.

"A few days later this younger son packed all his belongings and moved to a distant land, and there he wasted all his money in wild living. About the time his money ran out, a great famine swept over the land, and he began to starve. He persuaded a local farmer to hire him, and the man sent him into his fields to feed the pigs. The young man became so hungry that even the pods he was feeding the pigs looked good to him. But no one gave him anything.

"When he finally came to his senses, he said to himself, 'At home

even the hired servants have food enough to spare, and here I am dying of hunger! I will go home to my father and say, "Father, I have sinned against both heaven and you, and I am no longer worthy of being called your son. Please take me on as a hired servant."'

"So he returned home to his father. And while he was still a long way off, his father saw him coming. Filled with love and compassion, he ran to his son, embraced him, and kissed him. His son said to him, 'Father, I have sinned against both heaven and you, and I am no longer worthy of being called your son.'

"But his father said to the servants, 'Quick! Bring the finest robe in the house and put it on him. Get a ring for his finger and sandals for his feet. And kill the calf we have been fattening. We must celebrate with a feast, for this son of mine was dead and has now returned to life. He was lost, but now he is found.' So the party began.

"Meanwhile, the older son was in the fields working. When he returned home, he heard music and dancing in the house, and he asked one of the servants what was going on. 'Your brother is back,' he was told, 'and your father has killed the fattened calf. We are celebrating because of his safe return.' "The older brother was angry and wouldn't go in. His father came out and begged him, but he replied, 'All these years I've slaved for you and never once refused to do a single thing you told me to. And in all that time you never gave me even one young goat for a feast with my friends. Yet when this son of yours comes back after squandering your money on prostitutes, you celebrate by killing the fattened calf!'

"His father said to him, 'Look, dear son, you have always stayed by me, and everything I have is yours. We had to celebrate this happy day. For your brother was dead and has come back to life! He was lost, but now he is found!'"

- Luke 15:1-32 (NLT)

Jesus told three parables in succession to show something magnificent about the heart of God. He spoke of a lost sheep, a lost coin and finally a lost son.

Here we see a magnificent portrayal of "God the Father".

- The one sheep out of the hundred matters greatly to him.

- The one silver coin out of the ten matters greatly to him.

- And the one son out of two matters greatly to him!

The famous "prodigal son" parable is worthy of a book in itself, as it portrays a father of such love and grace that it offends his other son.

 - It speaks of a father who loves so much that he forgives every conceivable offence that a son could commit against him.

 - It speaks of a father who longs for that wicked son to return.

 - It speaks of a father who celebrates with outrageous generosity when the wicked son does return.

 - It speaks of a father whose forgiveness is so complete that he restores every privilege and right to the son who had rejected it all.

This is the love of the Father that brought Jesus to earth and to the cross. It is a love that surely wins our love in return!

WALK IT:

For "younger sons"

If you have walked away from God like the younger son, you may believe that you have "burned your bridges"; that you can never live as a child of God again. Look again at the incredible Father – and come back!!

For "elder sons"

If you have written off anyone for walking away from God, look again at the incredible Father – and welcome them when you see them. Perhaps you can help them find their way back? When they do come back, join your Father's party and celebrate!!

For "shepherds"

If you know someone who has walked away from God, how about searching for them? If you find them, tell them about the incredible Father – so that they might come back!

MY "LIFE LESSON":

39: God values humility, not self-sufficiency

Then Jesus told this story to some who had great confidence in their own righteousness and scorned everyone else:

"Two men went to the Temple to pray. One was a Pharisee, and the other was a despised tax collector. The Pharisee stood by himself and prayed this prayer: 'I thank you, God, that I am not a sinner like everyone else. For I don't cheat, I don't sin, and I don't commit adultery. I'm certainly not like that tax collector! I fast twice a week, and I give you a tenth of my income.'

"But the tax collector stood at a distance and dared not even lift his eyes to heaven as he prayed. Instead, he beat his chest in sorrow, saying, 'O God, be merciful to me, for I am a sinner.' I tell you, this sinner, not the Pharisee, returned home justified before God. For those who exalt themselves will be humbled, and those who humble themselves will be exalted."

- Luke 18:9-14 (NLT)

The Pharisee was a religious and respected man. He had studied God's laws intently and worked hard at applying and teaching them. In the eyes of society, he was surely in a great place with God! But all of that was invalidated by his self-sufficient attitude: he believed he had *earned* a right standing with God.

The tax collector in contrast, was probably a man of questionable morality. In the eyes of society, he was a traitor to his nation and a corrupt person, so was surely far from God. But this man knew his desperate need for God's mercy; so he asked for it – and received it!

God knows exactly who we are outside of the work of the Cross – sinners needing redemption. We would be wise not to imagine that we are righteous because there are people who (we think) sin more than we do! When we come to God in honest humility, knowing our absolute need for his mercy and grace, we will find all we need in Jesus.

WALK IT:

For "Pharisees"

If you have been a believer for some time, it is possible that you have forgotten that you are an object of mercy, a trophy of God's grace. Perhaps you have got used to "normal church life", have some healthy spiritual disciples like regular prayer and Bible reading, and feel pretty good about yourself... certainly better than "those out there"! If this attitude has sneaked into your heart, you can be confident that "those out there" sense it – and it could keep them from the very grace that saved you! Ask God to wash those attitudes away, reminding you of his incredible grace to you – so that you can humbly and kindly help others to find that same grace.

For "tax collectors"

If you have been looked down on – maybe even insulted – by pious or even arrogant religious types, this chapter is good news for you! God is not impressed by their self-righteousness. He knows who they really are, needing his grace just as much as you! All he wants from you is for you to come humbly to him for his grace and mercy.

Perhaps you have developed a picture of God that looks like those religious ones – and this is keeping you from him. Allow this message from Jesus to reveal the grace of God that is freely available to us all!

MY "LIFE LESSON":

40: God paid the highest price to rescue mankind from their sin

He walked away, about a stone's throw, and knelt down and prayed, "Father, if you are willing, please take this cup of suffering away from me. Yet I want your will to be done, not mine." Then an angel from heaven appeared and strengthened him. He prayed more fervently, and he was in such agony of spirit that his sweat fell to the ground like great drops of blood.

- Luke 22:41-44 (NLT)

The trial, flogging and crucifixion of Jesus was the most brutal way to die – but taking the sin of mankind upon himself was actually the most painful experience Jesus had to endure. The prospect of the impending agony was so horrific that Jesus in his humanity asked to be excused from it. Embracing it was so intense that he literally sweated blood.

Some think that God does not care about them; they clearly have not been gripped by the immense gravity and agony of the Cross of Christ! *There is surely no greater expression of love towards us!*

There is also another *vital* lesson to learn here: there was – and there still is – no other way to redeem mankind. As Jesus asked to be spared the agony of the cross, he effectively asked for another way of salvation to be provided. The answer was – and still is – "no, there is no other way". The cross was the only possible solution, so Jesus went to the cross.

John recorded a conversation with Jesus that has offended many:

"Don't let your hearts be troubled. Trust in God, and trust also in me. There is more than enough room in my Father's home. If this were not so, would I have told you that I am going to prepare a place for you? When everything is ready, I will come and get you, so that you will always be with me where I am. And you know the way to where I am going."

91

"No, we don't know, Lord," Thomas said. "We have no idea where you are going, so how can we know the way?"

Jesus told him, "I am the way, the truth, and the life. No one can come to the Father except through me."

- John 14:1-6 (NLT)

It is highly likely that this offends you, or some people you love. As we face the offence, we must face a harsh reality: that truth is truth even when we don't like it.

For followers of other religious systems, please realise that if this offends yours, know that this similarly offends *all* religious systems – including the Jewish Law given by God to Moses! Religious systems generally teach about God, righteousness and sinfulness, but the death and resurrection of Jesus Christ is not a religious system – *it is the means provided by God for all people to be redeemed from the sinful state that keeps them apart from him.*

If there was ever an offence to be wrestled through, this is it! Wrestle... pray... fight every battle that it takes to get through it, and embrace the way of salvation that God is offering you!

WALK IT:

Walking towards Jesus

If you have never embraced God's offer of forgiveness and sonship through the work of the cross of Christ, this is the "ultimate walk"! The decision to put our faith in Jesus, to embrace his offer of forgiveness and to entrust our lives into his hands is the decision that changes everything!

If you have a "big question" or two that is hindering you from putting your faith in Jesus, find a mature believer and get answers to your questions... or get hold of a book that clarifies the Gospel... or do a course such as the Alpha Course. *Do whatever it takes; you will not regret it!*

Walking towards others

Can you remember people who helped you "walk towards Jesus"? Let's do likewise! Let's help them fight through the barriers of questions, offences and doubts. There is surely no higher achievement than to help someone find their way to Jesus!!

MY "LIFE LESSON":